# The Day the World Ends

*poems by*

# Helen Weil

*Finishing Line Press*
Georgetown, Kentucky

# The Day the World Ends

## ACKNOWLEDGMENTS

I want to thank my family, especially my dad, for encouraging me to write.
Dad, I still remember you keeping and framing a (very bad) poem I wrote
for you when I was little. Without your support, I wouldn't have had the
courage to get to where I am now.

I also want to thank my friends Erica and Alberto for always being willing to
dive headfirst into the worlds I dream up.

To all of my loved ones, you are and forever will be my driving force.
Everything I do is for you and because of you, and these poems are no
exception. Thank you.

Publisher: Leah Huete de Maines
Editor: Christen Kincaid
Cover Art: Erica Gerlach
Author Photo: Alberto Villifan
Cover Design: Elizabeth Maines McCleavy


Order online: www.finishinglinepress.com
also available on amazon.com

Author inquiries and mail orders:
Finishing Line Press
PO Box 1626
Georgetown, Kentucky 40324
USA

# Contents

## Hope, I (Call...)

when everyone breathes their last
I hope there's no bang, no whimper
just everything slowing to a stop
I hope the wind blows sweet song through open windows
unperturbed by our mass stillness
I hope the animals know nothing of our disappearance
gingerly stumbling back onto forgotten territory
I hope there's no fighting
no mourning
no sound of struggle or strife
I hope our ending is quiet
we deserve a gentle goodnight

## Hope, II (...and Response)

I want more for us than a gentle ending
I want us to go down laughing singing celebrating
with cake and top-shelf bourbon
fireworks over the Thames and Seine
confetti in Times Square
and when the dust settles
I hope the empty streets are painted
in all our favorite colors

## Hope, III

the day the world ends
I hope I walk to work in my favorite dress
I'll smile at my neighbors and cherish the birdsong
I hope the sun shines warm on my face

I hope I tell my students I love them
read them books and make them eat their veggies
stay with them until they fall asleep
tuck soft plushies into little hands

I hope I call my sister and make her laugh
I hope the neighborhood coffee shop isn't busy
I hope the walk is filled with good music

I hope I savor the hot water I bathe in
and put on my softest pajamas
I hope I fall asleep quickly
and dream of warmth and soft things—
my sister's laughter
little hands held in mine—
when the sun burns out
and the tide rises
and we enter the long dark night.

I hope I spend my last day not knowing it's my last
and I hope I spend it living

# Act I: The End
*(pronounced like "Beginning")*

**I Am**

there is no imagining the end.

the nothingness before the Big Bang
the inky blackness at the bottom of the ocean
a silent, lightless night
a thousand stars snuffed at once

humanity is light and noise
movement and creation and destruction
handprints on cave walls
bodies preserved and graves marked
dancing around crackling fires
storytelling around the spindle

I once learned that music is found in every culture on earth
it's in our DNA
who could imagine an Earth without music?
humans without song and dance?

the end cannot be fathomed because we are not part of it
but I am.

the sun rose on a silent planet
billions went to sleep—
only I woke up

when I scream shout sing
my response is the howling wolves and cawing crows

this is Earth, silent, still
without humanity

I am alone.

## Mourning

I stumble first to my childhood best friend's house. the route is
muscle memory.

I never left home, but she did. buoyed by dreams larger than life,
she soared close to the sun—but her mother grew sick, so she
went home and her wings were clipped.

she slept in her childhood bed. the master bedroom, she swore,
was haunted.
her own bedroom, pink and fully of girlish keepsakes, had no
such burden.

her front door is locked but I know where the key is hidden. I let
myself in and am hit with a smell I know without knowing.

I know where I will find her body.
I don't go looking for it.
I give her no funeral, but I eulogize her on the sidewalk.
I search the garage for dusty chalk from a bygone era and I draw
her a garden.

she could see it from her bedroom window
if she would just get up.

her curtains do not move, and after a while,
I walk back down silent streets
back to an empty house
without her,
or anyone else.

**To the other half of me**

I can't remember the blip in time when you weren't around
that stilted half-life doesn't matter
I was born knowing you

so close you were behind me
I figured we'd go together, too
twin funerals, twin graves
like matching Easter dresses
like two sets of keys to our first car
like identical presents on Christmas morning

I never fathomed having to live without you
without being your sister
I don't know how to be

## Stranded

matter is never created nor destroyed
but the people I love are gone
I am alone forgotten lost

I scream myself raw
split the skin of my knuckles
acting on white-hot rage and a hairpin trigger

when I burn out
I sit in the carnage and try to repent
but the gods seem to have left me, too

## Go On

I dream of flying
off of very tall buildings
letting the ocean current carry me out
crashing a car with the pedal to the floor
lying down and not getting back up

at the ledge
the shore
the driver's seat
the forest floor

I find nothing but a simple truth
I have too much living left to do
and a long time before I can sleep

# Act II: The Journey

## Freedom

I have never known such freedom

I sleep in a penthouse apartment
a luxury hotel room
a parked school bus

I swim in public pools
bathe in lakes
drink from rivers

I take food from the backs of restaurants
clothes from fancy department stores
makeup and jewelry from the outlet mall

I play dress-up
twirl in lacy dresses and red-bottom heels
cut my hair and try on wigs

I smash windows and cars
pick flowers and locks
drink top-shelf liquor and bitter campfire coffee

I decide I'll go see the country
in a sports car, a camper,
an ambulance

I floor it down empty highways
blow through stop signs and careen around curves
drive so fast I can forget that the traffic lights don't work anymore

joy tastes different after tragedy

**To the love of another life**

in another life
I might've left when you asked me
to run away with you

I might've bought that ring
taken you to that little chapel
taken you home

I might've gone down easier, then
if you were there to hold me through the night

## The plains

I travel far.
the roads are empty, long and snaking
the plains stretch before me
tall wheat bending in the breeze like ocean waves

I stumble through abandoned farmhouses
horses running wild in the overgrown fields
silent machinery with rusted teeth
crops rot where they fall
no hands catch what they cultivated

crows pick through the wreckage
I am a scavenger, too
picking up discarded cans and soft sweaters
the throw blanket off the back of the couch

I sleep in no bedrooms—
they are all occupied
I bury no bodies—
they are already at rest

what cold misery would the dirt be
when the alternative is feather-stuffed pillows
hand-sewn quilts
the head of your lover on your chest?

the plains are empty
wide and vast
there is nothing left for me.

## Quiet

I used to like the quiet
I was always searching for peace
sunny afternoons at the lake
stormy mornings in bed
folding laundry at work while the children slept

it's easy to want the fleeting things
harder to love what's always there
I miss the noise
I miss the screech of city traffic
I miss the haze of a brightly-lit downtown
I miss hearing another's voice

I find myself wishing on the too-bright stars
just one more day
one more minute at a long stoplight
one more drink at the corner coffee shop
one more family dinner

the nights are longer and darker
than I thought imaginable
and sleep does not come easily

I abandon my quest for freedom
instead I begin to hunt for answers
why me?
why not them?

## University

I camp on pleather dining hall booths
the soda machine spits crystallized syrupy gunk
curdled milk drips off the cereal bar

above me,
there are floors and floors
rooms and rooms of narrow bunk beds
like shelves in a crypt
in windows, I see flickering string lights and wilting plants
I cannot bear the weight of all their futures
snuffed out

I search for my answer
in the Chemistry Hall
then Biology
Earth Science
Engineering
Philosophy

science and math have no answer for me
instead I find it in the shelves of the library
a dozen imagined endings, cataloged in neat rows

ocean swells, hurricanes, earthquakes, eclipses
technology that knows war as intimately as we do
judgment day, rapture, apocalypse
sickness, radiation, pain
anger, consequence, accident

I realize that it doesn't matter
there was no way of preparing
and no way of repairing what we've done
no going back

the only truth is
we met our inevitable end
and I am alone in the aftermath.

*(Excerpt from a book unread:*
*There will be no reprieve of daylight*
*No sunbaked concrete or warm breeze*
*But the night is cool and gentle*
*The stars shine like shattered sunlight*
*Tiny fractals of the fire we used to know*
*The tide comes in with the darkened moon*
*Waveless, glass-still*
*The world sleeps in silence*
*We won't miss the light*
*Promise)*

## Outbreak

winter comes swiftly, an open palm between the shoulder blades. I use a road atlas to find a shuttered ski lodge and there I learn to use an ax. I build fires in the foyer fireplace, smokey and sappy and cedar-scented.

in the blinding white day, I shuffle from room to room. winter finds its way inside. the cold seeps through the walls, and windows shatter from the plummeting temperatures. I gather blankets and pillows and robes and fuzzy slippers and tiny bottles of shampoo.

in the long black night, I stay in the light of the fireplace. the wind howls and the forest animals answer.

I find books. flashlights. chlorine for a hot tub that's gone grimy and green. a ballroom with a grand piano and a little disco ball. paints and easels and bottles of wine. boxes of Christmas decorations.

in the lost and found, I find mittens and hats and scarves and balaclavas, a digital camera, a gold locket, a beaded friendship bracelet. I take it all.

I read and paint and decorate and dance and bang on the keys. I go out in search of the best pine tree I can find. I chop it down and drag it into the ballroom and hang glass ornaments from its branches.

I have Christmas dinner during a blizzard—a can of green beans and a bottle of champagne.

it's always dark. I'm always sleeping. I'm always freezing. it's hard to keep the fire going. I don't know how long the food will last. I wish to fly south like a migratory bird. I wish to lay down in the snow and fall asleep one last time.

I haunt the halls of this wretched place. time is thick and
heavy in my hands.

eventually, the long winter ends and tiny green shoots break
through the frozen ground.

I take the embers from my dying fire and toss them on the
velveteen carpet. by the time I'm down the mountain, the
whole place is ablaze. I finally feel warm.

## Rebirth

I am brought to my knees by the roar of waterfalls,
overflowing with snowmelt
with stiff fingers I wash away winter's silence

shivering and blue
I lay my withered body out on the rocks
my face pinkens in the desperate spring sunshine

I am made of something fragile today
worn down like these old buildings
one misstep away from shattering

but the breeze is gentle and the sun is warm
I push on through
and pray that I'll be stronger tomorrow

## The coast

I always dreamed of moving to a little town on the coast.
somewhere the pace of life is slower and the ocean
is a constant heartbeat like the one I pressed my ear to
every time my father held me.

in another daydream, I moved to a big city
and learned to love the twinkling lights
as much as I once loved the stars.
in yet another, I never know a sky that isn't full of constellations.

how many versions of myself will I have to bury?
how many small deaths will I feel before the real thing comes?

I find the sea and play pretend
in a shuttered vacation house.
I find the city, but by then
the lights have gone dark, and the stars shine
brighter than I ever saw before, even out in the countryside.

the stars were never their brightest for us.
they waited until we left, giving their light
to the dolphins splashing through the mirror-still water,
the eagles riding the air currents,
the slow-moving sloths and waddling brown bears.

the constellations were never ours to name.
we are made of stardust and maybe
we thought that gave us the right,
but we were just after-images of greater glory,
small specks in a story
much too big for us to understand.

we thought the universe cared about our plans.
what a joke.

**Telescope**

I find a deserted house
with a 'for sale' sign out front
big windows look over the empty, endless desert
I am a thousand miles from home

hastily emptied
I still see glimmers
of the life once lived here

I find a child's bedroom
a few glow-in-the-dark stars stubbornly remain
stuck to the ceiling, painted over in white
a constellation takes shape above me
I stand on the empty bed frame and trace it

I think of the astronauts who made it to the Moon
temporary guests with illusions of grandeur
and dreams of settling somewhere new

why would we ever want to leave our paradise
our oasis
in the empty, endless desert
there's nothing out there for us
no sunlight or soft grass or cool water

just an emptiness we weren't meant to know

**Sweet music**

shortly before the electric grid died out, I found the movie theater where I worked away my teenage summers. I climbed up into the booth and turned on the big projector, and I got to be a part of the last human story ever told.

ghosts danced on a silver screen, larger than life, bigger than my memories. I savored every sound I'd started to forget.

I know voices are one of the first things to go—when death took my mother's hand, it was the first piece of her I lost. I remember the warmth of her hugs, the smell of her perfume, but my memories of her play out like a silent film.

I can't lose anyone else.

when the cities finally went dark, I picked up
instruments, walkmans, boomboxes.
I think of my father's favorite song, volume cranked up
on the car radio;
children's lullabies on a CD in the daycare;
my friend's hand on piano keys, playing something classical,
practicing for a recital.

some days, I feel less than human. then I find a new cassette and I hear them again.

there you are.
I missed you.

## Green

in college, I took an elective course in paleontology
on the final exam there was a trick question:
*what part of us will remain the longest after we're gone?*
the answer wasn't our skulls our femurs our teeth or jaws
nor the tiny little bones that make up our fingers
fossilized and preserved for some other species to find
the answer was our tools
our plastic and metal things
all that which we shaped with fragile, temporary hands

but it's been a while now
the signs of us are starting to decay

weeds push through concrete, burying the rock under rich soil
steel frame buildings become rusted skeletons the kudzu climbs

the world is so green again
unfamiliar, unblemished, whole
I wish I didn't miss the gray

## To someone from another time

dear friend,
in my dreams, I love you
enough to bring you back
when I wake, I find you
in every lovely thing
I hope when I see you again
it's like no time has passed at all

# Act III: Going Home

**Narcissus**

lately I haven't been recognizing myself
the woman I see in dirty mirrors and still ponds
she's as wild as the forest creatures

in my dreams I'm still human
whole and unwearied
in my nightmares I'm unrecognizable
those I've lost come back
just to sneer at the animal I've become
it's not my fault, I plead
look at what you left me with

in the morning I apologize for the horrible things I think
they're just the ramblings of a dying species

## Pitstop

animals don't run from me anymore
or the headlights of whatever vehicle I've stolen this week

(cars are getting harder to find
the gas won't last much longer
and the roads are buckled and ragged)

the animals are right—
there isn't much to fear anymore
our human mightiness has crumbled in time

that isn't to say I can't find signs of what we used to be
I have seen the country but I'm fading fast
I am coming home now and the sights are becoming familiar

the daycare where I used to work when the world still spun
feels unnatural without children running down the halls
the old building's purpose surgically removed

the sun cuts thin beams through dirty windows
smiling on a faded mural
its colors drained by time

my memories are similarly shaded
I remember tight hugs and echoing laughter
but their faces are faded

I find moth-eaten baby blankets
a playground, a dozen toy cars swallowed up by the grass
dew-speckled clovers and tiny toads hopping among them

there is peace here
it's quiet
I rest for a while.

# Home

I never really gave thought to my funeral
but I start to imagine it now
would I have liked flowers? wreaths?
lilacs, daisies, peonies?

I never wanted it in a stuffy funeral home
I don't want to be seen waxen and stiff,
dressed by unfamiliar hands
no, I want to be remembered better

I want sunlight and open sky
a soft forest floor
my bones becoming entwined with the tree roots

mostly, I just want to go home
and find the pieces of me buried in the garden
I'd lay down in the dirt and let the church bells wash over me
remind me of when I was young and it was summer
my windows open, curtains shifting in the soft breeze,
the cicadas were loud and the birds were, too,
and the church bells rang every evening at five o'clock
time stretched so long back then

I wish I didn't take for granted the safety of those four blue
walls
I wish I didn't waste my childhood wishing to grow up
I wish I was still young—
still playing in the backyard with my sister and the
neighborhood kids
waiting to be called home for dinner

the church bells went silent long ago
but they still call me home

## Let Go

I am no stranger to tragedy
I knew loss so young it stitched itself
into the lining of my soul

despite this, I do not know how to let go
I hold tight to everything I love
leaving bruises and my fingernails bloody

how foolish to think that I had any control over when people
leave
how hard it is to understand that love is fleeting
but no less grand without forever

I have found home in people and places and things
my friends' easy laughter
the matchbox-sized dorm I lived in at eighteen
my sister's familiar brown eyes
the dip in the living room couch
a tight hug from my father

so I know loss
but I also know love
and I am beginning to understand that forever
is a pot of gold beyond what is already
a magnificent rainbow

they loved me all their lives
and I will love them for the rest of mine
promise

## End

when it finally comes for me, too,
I sigh in relief.

a hand is offered,
warm and worn,
the hand of my
            mother         father            grandmother
                                   sister                    best friend
I take it.

I am led back to a suburban house in 2008
cartoons on the basement TV
my baby sister,
blunt bangs and missing teeth,
passes me an apple slice

we play with Barbies until dinner time
spaghetti, plain,
carrot sticks and glasses of milk
steam obscures the kitchen window
it's getting dark so early now

Dad reads a book to us
a daughter under each arm
he slides a bookmark in it,
saving the ending for another night

I trail my fingers over the lumpy paint on the railing
drag my feet over compacted carpet
run my nails over outdated wallpaper
Dad puts her to bed first
I can hear the soft goodnights through the wall

then it's my turn
I'm tucked into my too-big bed
swaddled in hand-me-down blankets
my dad turns out the light

as I drift off,
safe and warm and loved,
I am home.

I find no afterlife
just the gentle, dark night.

**Helen Weil** is a poet, writer, and educator from the Chicago suburbs who is equally fond of ghost stories and love stories. She studied Psychology and Creative Writing at the University of Minnesota and went on to earn an M.Ed. in Early Childhood Education. Her poems and short stories have appeared in the *Dalliances Anthology* (Cupid's Arrow Publishing, 2025), *Saturday Evening Post, The Tower, Kalopsia Lit, Firework Stories, Fleeting Daze Magazine,* and *Seaglass Literary Magazine.* She formerly served as Head Prose Judge for the Letters Home Collection. Helen currently resides in Minneapolis, Minnesota, with her cat Bunny. When she's not writing, Helen can be found at the local movie theater.

www.ingramcontent.com/pod-product-compliance
Lightning Source LLC
Chambersburg PA
CBHW022046080426
42734CB00009B/1255